ON
LITERATURE
TODAY

VAN WYCK BROOKS

HAS WRITTEN:

NEW ENGLAND: INDIAN SUMMER, 1865–1915
THE FLOWERING OF NEW ENGLAND
THE LIFE OF EMERSON
THE ORDEAL OF MARK TWAIN
THE PILGRIMAGE OF HENRY JAMES
EMERSON AND OTHERS
THREE ESSAYS ON AMERICA
America's Coming-of-Age
Letters and Leadership
The Literary Life in America
SKETCHES IN CRITICISM

Published by
E. P. DUTTON & CO., INC.

ON LITERATURE TODAY

BY

VAN WYCK BROOKS

1941
NEW YORK
E. P. DUTTON & CO., INC.

AMERICAN BOOK—STRATFORD PRESS, INC., NEW YORK

NOTE

This address was delivered at the inauguration
of Dr. George N. Shuster as President of Hunter
College, New York, October 10th, 1940.

ON
LITERATURE
TODAY

ON LITERATURE TODAY

I HAVE BEEN asked to speak on the state of our literature today. We live in a very unhappy world at present, a time of great confusion, and the public has a right to expect from its poets and thinkers some light on the causes of our problems and the way to a better future. Few writers, I think, at present, are living up to these expectations. But still the belief in literature persists, because so many writers in the past have performed their true public function. "In literature alone," said Leopardi, "the regeneration of our country can have a substantial beginning." This may seem a large claim, and yet there is some truth in it, for, as Ibsen said, "Except as afterwards invented"—invented, that is, by thinking minds—"the conscious guiding principle is never present in the general sentiment of the people." The world can only be changed by desires, but we are always desiring things, and only ideas can make desires effective; and so the minds that invent and express have a powerful influence over us. What then is literature doing for us in these perplexing times? And if it is not doing more and better, what are the reasons for this?

Literature at all times is a very complex phenomenon. When you see it in perspective, historically, it seems simple enough. We know what we call the Victorian age. As it appears in the histories, it is like the map of a country, all one colour, with novelists, poets and essayists of various sizes, corresponding to towns and cities, dotted over the surface, united by currents of thought as clearly represented as rivers and railroads. But if one had lived in that age, it would all have seemed very different. An age is a chaos while one is living in it, and the past would be a chaos also if it were not interpreted for us. Besides, it is difficult to understand living writers because they are involved in our problems, which we cannot solve for ourselves. To generalize about the present is therefore a hazardous undertaking, although we are compelled to undertake it. All manner of writers are living in the world, and if, confining oneself to America, one thinks of talent, and even genius, the present seems to me beyond all question one of the brilliant epochs. In literary capacity, in vigour of style, in the number of our novelists, poets and critics, we are obviously in the midst of a revival; and I am only quoting foreign writers, English, Irish, French, Scandinavian, Russian, when I say that never before, outside this country, wherever books are read, have American writers been so influential. But, aside from this question of talent, there is another question, implied in my quotations from Leopardi and Ibsen. Among these brilliant writers, where does one find the "conscious guiding principle"? How far do they contribute to "regenerate the country"? Let the Russian writer Chekhov reply to these questions. "Lift the robe of our muse and you will find within an empty void." Chekhov said this fifty years ago, and perhaps it expresses your feeling about our current literature. You may agree with a further observation which I have found in Chekhov's Letters: "Let me remind you that the writers who, we say, are for all time, or are simply good, and who intoxicate us, have one common and very important characteristic. They are going towards something and are summoning you towards it, too, and you feel, not with your mind, but with your whole

being, that they have some object . . . The best of
them are realists and paint life as it is, but, through
every line's being soaked in the consciousness of an
object, you feel, besides life as it is, the life which
ought to be, and that captivates you. And we? We
paint life as it is, but beyond that—nothing at all.
We have neither immediate nor remote aims, and
in our soul there is a great empty space."

I quote this long passage because it suggests the
dominant note of our epoch. We have, to be sure,
many writers who do not convey this impression,
writers who make us feel what ought to be and for
whom life is noble and important. In Robert Frost,
in Lewis Mumford, to mention two of these, one
feels a joyous confidence in human nature, an
abounding faith in the will, a sense of the heroic
in the human adventure, good will, the leaven of
existence. All good things seem possible as one
reads these writers. I remember a remark of John
Butler Yeats, the father of the Irish poet. Thirty
years ago, in New York, I used to see him every
day, and one day he spoke of an old friend of his
in Dublin, a judge who had retired from the
bench. When someone asked this judge what remained in his mind, what had most deeply im-

pressed him, during his fifty years in the criminal courts, his answer was, "The goodness of human nature." The grand old Yeats, who also loved his species, quoted this with a smile of agreement, for although he did not take an easy view of life, he felt that a seasoned magistrate knew whereof he spoke. I have never forgotten this remark, and I have always felt that literature, if it is to carry out its function, must contain this germ of faith, and that the greatest literature has always done so. The writers who retain this faith are what we call idealists. Robert Frost and Lewis Mumford—let me repeat their names, and there are many others—stand in our time for this position. In them one feels the power of the healthy will. Whenever I think of them, I remember Whitman's line, "Allons, the road is before us."

This mood of health, will, courage, faith in human nature, is the dominant mood in the history of literature. It was the mood of Homer, and writers will always return to it, as water always rises to the level of its source. It is the warp of literature —the rest is the woof. But this is not the mood of the last two decades, and it seems as if these writers had lost the day, as if the poet Yeats were right in saying (although perhaps in quite a different sense),——

> The best lack all conviction, while the worst
> Are full of passionate intensity.

A mood of desperate unhappiness reigns in the world, and this is marked especially in most of the writers. Have you thought how strange it is that so much of the world swallowed Spengler whole? ——and I do not deny that Spengler was a very great genius, I do not deny the reality of his intuitions. The temperamental cards of our time are all stacked in favour of despair, and a somewhat sterile despair. One error that an optimist makes destroys his whole case, while a pessimist can get away with murder. It seems as if our writers passively wallowed in misery, calling it fate; as if the most powerful writers, from James Joyce to Hemingway, from Eliot of *The Waste Land* to Eugene O'Neill and Theodore Dreiser, were bent on proving that life is a dark little pocket. Influence in literature goes with intensity. The intense minds, good or evil, are those that wield the power; and the genius that has moulded the mind of the present is almost wholly destructive; and even where,

as in many cases, these writers are fighting for social justice, they still picture life as hardly worth
the trouble of fighting for it. Their tone is cynical,
bleak, hard-boiled, hard-bitten, and life for them
is vain, dark and empty, the plaything, in Theodore Dreiser's phrase, of "idle rocking forces" or
currents of material interest. What did Joyce's
Ulysses say if not that life is a bad joke? What do
our novelists say if not that nothing good exists,
that only the ugly is real, the perverted, the dis-
torted? You know the picture of life you find in
the novels of William Faulkner, Dos Passos,
James T. Farrell and so many others, who carry
the day with their readers because they are writers
of great power. They seem to delight in kicking
their world to pieces, as if civilization were all a
pretence and everything noble a humbug. There
are teachers and psychologists who back them up.
Only the other day I was reading a well-known
psychologist who made two statements that he
took for granted: 1, Men have always known that
the romantic picture of love is false; 2, That
which portrays the neurotic and defeated in human nature is closer to truth than that which pic-
tures the aspirations of men. Love is a lie, in short,

and the only realities are defeat and failure. This mood of incredulity and despair has penetrated millions of minds, and one finds it in the most unexpected places. There are people, educated people, who really think that Plutarch's heroes were humbugs, that Plutarch was pulling the wool over his readers' eyes when he pretended that heroes had ever existed. For these people, and they are many, all the closets are full of skeletons, for them even Diogenes was optimistic. What a gullible fellow Diogenes was—imagine wasting one's time, going about with a lantern, looking for an honest man, as if such a thing were to be conceived of! Not long ago I was talking with a distinguished professor about Eugene O'Neill's play *Mourning Becomes Electra*. He said that O'Neill had given the only truthful picture of New England, the New England not only of the present but of the past—that Cambridge and Concord a hundred years ago were just like this village in the play, whited sepulchres, full of dead men's bones. As for the old New England writers, who presented a different picture, they were all hypocrites and liars. So far has this iron of incredulity entered into the modern soul.

What this all means is seldom discussed in the critical writing of the present. Most of our critical writing deals with technical questions, and technical novelty, as it seems to me, is almost the only virtue it demands or praises. Not whether a writer contributes to life, but whether he excels in some new trick, is the question that is usually asked. It is their formal originality that has given prestige to writers like Joyce, Eliot and Gertrude Stein; and perhaps this is natural in an age of technics. But how can we ignore the larger questions involved in this drift of the modern mind? It seems to me it represents the "death-drive," as certain psychologists call it, the will to die that is said to exist side by side in our minds with the will to live. Defeat and unhappiness can reach a point where we accept them and embrace them and rejoice in our enervation and disintegration. And whether we rejoice in it or not, this literature is disintegrating. "All that is ugly," Nietzsche said, "weakens and afflicts man. It reminds him of deterioration, of danger and of impotence. He actually suffers loss of power by it. The effect of ugliness," Nietzsche continues, "can be measured by the dynamometer. Whenever man is depressed, he has a sense of the proximity of something ugly. His sense of power, his will to power, his courage, his pride—they decrease with the ugly, they increase with the beautiful." That is what I mean by suggesting that all these writers represent the death-drive. And if, with their technical virtues, they destroy our faith, our will to make the world worth living in, we cannot let their influence go unchallenged.

Now, I have an instinctive will to believe in writers. Deep down below the level where I agree or disagree with them, I like and respect them because they are writers. In less expansive moods, I admit that there are rattlesnake writers, rhinoceros, hyena, jackal writers. There are literary Hitlers and Mussolinis, who are as useful to the race as a large and active copperhead in August. But writers, as a class, as I have known them, are sensitive, scrupulous men, lovers of justice and full of good will for other people. They are almost all idealists by instinct. And so, when I see great numbers of writers bent, as they seem to be, on destroying life, I ask myself, What are the reasons for it? Why do they see only the ugly in life? Why are they so cynical and fatalistic? And are they to blame for this, or are we to blame—we, all of us, society, the world we live in? Creative minds, of all minds, are those that naturally love life most. Obviously, these writers have been disappointed.

It is a commonplace that all these writers have expressed the state of mind of a world between wars. Thirty years ago, when I began to write, the future was an exciting and hopeful vista. Everyone believed in evolution, as a natural social process. We took the end for granted. Mankind was marching forward, and the only questions were of ways and means. I do not need to say how far the first world-war destroyed this happy vista. The young and sensitive minds who grew up in its shadow were utterly disillusioned by what they saw. They felt they had been betrayed, and, as evil triumphed, they came to feel that nothing else was real. This was the case all over our world, and the triumph of reactionary forces, in the years that followed, has gone very far to confirm this impression. We have witnessed every day the success of the powers of evil, that have bragged and bullied their way towards the rule of the world. Everything good has been pushed to the wall, and even five years ago Bertrand Russell, speaking of England, said that no one could think of reform any longer, no one could think of anything but the approaching menace, the threat of these conquering forces that have darkened the world. If, in this respect, we are relatively fortunate, our writers have shared this world-depression; and their cynicism has other local causes. The optimistic picture of our life that prevailed in the last generation led to a reaction that was automatic. It was too good to be true; and as Howells, for instance, could not bear to look at the ugly things in life, the ugly things in life became an obsession with the novelists who followed. A similar reaction took place in the sphere of language. The obscenity and profanity of many of our writers seems to me as childish as the prudery of Howells; but Howells was prudish, and much of his generation was prudish, and this was bound to lead to what I call inverted prudery. Just so we had our "debunking" biographies, in reaction against the writers who drew the veil over the faults of their heroes; and in other ways too our civilization is reaping its whirlwinds. A few years ago, as a publishers' reader, I ran through a novel every day by some young man or woman who had grown up in the West or the South. They could not seem to

ON LITERATURE TODAY

forgive the towns they were born in—just to escape from these towns and tell the world how ugly, false and brutal they were seemed to be almost the motive of these writers in living. I think our generation will be remembered as the one in which everyone hated, often without visible reason, the town in which he was born. And the writers of whom I am speaking were obsessed with ugly memories, ugly as to material things and mostly as to spiritual. And I thought, Well, these towns were not founded with sensitive types in view. They were founded by aggressive men who were seeking an outlet for their primitive forces, and now the sensitive types have appeared and demanded their place in the sun, and their world is not ready to receive them. You know how Thomas Wolfe describes his country: "More land, more wooden houses, more towns, hard and raw and ugly . . . Ugly disorder and meanness." The moral of his novel is the moral of hundreds of other American novels: "The great masculine flower of gentleness, courage and honour died in a foul tangle." We are getting in this generation the reports of writers who have seen nothing else but this rawness and hardness. And we are getting also the reports of the excluded, the children of our newly arrived foreign population, many of whom have seen little else in all their lives but the slums and mean streets of monstrous cities, who have often known here little but slights and indignity. How far, for them, has America been the promised land of which we heard so much before the war?

It is the reports of all these classes that we are getting in our fiction—the excluded, the disinherited and the hypersensitive types who have grown up in our less developed regions. Worst of all, we have been getting the reports of expatriates, whose prestige of late has been immense. And when I say expatriates, I mean the word in our sense—not the sense it has come to have in connection with refugee intellectuals. The expatriates to whom I refer are those who have broken with their group-life, by choice, on grounds of taste and taste alone. The prestige of Henry James rose with that of Ezra Pound, Gertrude Stein, Eliot and various others. These writers, as writers, have great integrity, and they have made discoveries, both literary and psychological, that entitle them to much of their position; and you may say that where one lives is a purely personal question. Is it possible to lay down rules about it? Certainly many writers have lived outside their country and served their country or the world better by so doing. Ibsen lived for forty years abroad, and he said he had never seen his home so clearly as from a distance and during his absence. But I do not think this is true for Americans, perhaps because our roots are not so deep as the roots of men of older countries. When we leave our country we are apt to leave our roots behind us, and we fail to develop roots in any other country; and what this means is that we miss the deeper experiences that give us a mature point of view. Missing these experiences, we live on the surface, and, having evaded life because we cannot master it, we end by denying its importance —we end by denying the importance of all the primary things of life. You know how all these writers ridicule provinciality. But much of what they call provincial is basic in every civilization. No country could survive for six months without it. To escape from provinciality is good, provided we make distinctions; but, besides provinciality of place, there is also "time-provinciality," as Professor Whitehead calls it. This is the illusion that to be modern is worth all the other virtues; and the great effort of these writers is to represent the last minute, as if to keep up with the mode were more important than any of the great realities of life and death. They make much of technical questions because they have little to say otherwise, and they sneer at the great writers of the past, as Henry James used to say that Tolstoy was not worth reading, as Eliot prefers to Milton a dozen obscure metaphysical poets. To exalt the inferior over the great, in the name of their technical virtues, is a way of defending their own weakness; and Gertrude Stein has reduced their position to the last absurdity. In her theory of aesthetics, neither thought nor feeling matters. Nothing counts but the word-pattern, and the greatest thing in life is a nursery-jingle.

You know this is infantile, and in fact it seems to me that most of our current literature is written by adolescent minds. Mencken has remained a boy. The brag and bluster of Hemingway speak for a boy,—certainly a very gallant boy; so do Thomas Wolfe's poetic gropings; so does the cult of *Huckleberry Finn*, uniquely a book of boys, for boys, by a boy. Our novelists seldom picture developed types; and, if Eliot exalts the minor poets over the major poets, is it not because he does not feel the major emotional problems? If this is the case, what is the reason but a lack of the sort of attachments, to the family, to the soil, to public life, that develop the sense of responsibility and, with this, maturity of mind? Let me add that the writers I have mentioned have felt this problem; they have all, in one way or another, struggled with it, and that is why, among us, they are eminent writers. But even if they, the eminent, are adolescent—because of the conditions of our time —what shall we say of the rank and file, who are boys without the genius? The great cry of this age is that we should "face life;" but facing life means in many cases evading the most important elements of life. The world has seemed so difficult to writers, it has seemed so sinister and fearful, that to keep their personalities alive they have thrown the cargo over to save the ship. Their lives have been narrowed and desiccated, and they have remained emotionally shallow.

But, to return to their cynicism, does it really deny ideals? Is it not properly seen, rather, as a desperate affirmation of them? The depth of the

despair of the present is the measure of its defeated
expectation. It demands, it presupposes, the things
it denies. Our writers like to say that "free will" is
played out. They think they are determinists, but
they always turn out to be fatalists, and that is
quite a different matter. William James marked
the distinction. "The fatalistic argument," he
said, "is really no argument for simple determinism. There runs through it the sense of a force
which might make things otherwise from one mo-
ment to another, if it were only strong enough to
breast the tide. A person who feels the *impotence*
of free effort in this way has the acutest notion of
what is meant by it, and of its possible independ-
ent power. How else could he be so conscious of its
absence and of that of its effects? But genuine
determinism occupies a totally different ground:
not the *impotence*, but the *unthinkability* of free
will is what it affirms." There is the Asiatic atti-
tude, and one could never imagine an Asiatic writing as Faulkner writes, or Dos Passos, or Dreiser,
or Hemingway or any of our writers. It takes long
generations of disappointment, hundreds and thousands of years of disillusion, to produce the deter-
ministic frame of mind. The determinist is one

26

who has never had any expectations, but our American fatalism presupposes hope. It does not argue that free will does not exist; it merely affirms that the will is not effective. It pays the highest tribute to the will, for it says that life is meaningless and empty precisely because of this negation. The only unthinkable thing, for American minds, is that the will should not exist; and that is the reason why, when it is not effective, its impotence seems to Americans so overwhelming.

So it appears that the mood of these writers is a kind of inverted idealism. Their harsh incredulity is the measure of their potential faith; and when I think of the loose talk about "high ideals" that governed the general mind when I was a boy, and that went hand in hand with so many abuses, it seems to me that this turn of thought should prove in the end beneficial, creative of all that it misses. The ideal has often been maintained by those who have denied it in their youth; and, while there are no Saint Augustines in my generation, or any John Bunyans that I know of, I think the mind of the country, as a whole, has had its adolescence in our time—old as the sections were, the South, New England. It has gone through terrible growing pains, but the nation will be, in consequence, more mature. It is a good thing, surely, that young people now are so exacting, so wary of hypocrisy and humbug. And is there not a visible reaction against the defeatist mind, and against these parasites and air-plants, who have thriven in a discouraged world, as Spanish moss thrives on decaying trees? I see on all sides a hunger for affirmations, for a world without confusion, waste or groping, a world that is full of order and purpose, and for ourselves, in America, a chance to build it. When Europe too had its chance, and Americans were hankering for Europe, William James wrote, "Europe has been made what it is by men staying in their homes and fighting stubbornly, generation after generation, for all the beauty, comfort and order they have got. We must abide and do the same." Europe still has its chance, no doubt; but Europe is reaping whirlwinds far worse than ours and has lost the charm for us that it once possessed. It has thrown us back upon ourselves, and America has risen immensely in its power to charm us. Thousands of novels, biographies and histories, published in recent years, have shown us what multifarious strivings and failures and what multifarious victories lie behind us; and young writers now are settling in the remotest regions, determined to find them interesting or make them so. You never hear now of Greenwich Village, which used to be a haven for the exiles from Alabama and Kansas, the West and the South; and the reason you never hear of it is that the exiles have gone back to Alabama and to Kansas. They are founding schools in Iowa City and writing novels about Montana, and some are poet-farmers in Vermont. They are cultivating their roots where the seeds were sown, and where they are sure to yield their flowers and fruit.